Stoke-on-Trent

IN OLD PHOTOGRAPHS

A carte-de-visite photograph showing three local men wearing everyday clothes, c. 1890. The photographers, Barnard and Heilbronn, were active in Hanley between 1890 and 1900.

Stoke-on-Trent

IN OLD PHOTOGRAPHS

Compiled by
TIM CORUM *and* IAN LAWLEY

Sutton Publishing Limited
Phoenix Mill · Thrupp · Stroud
Gloucestershire · GL5 2BU

First published 1993
Reprinted 1994, 1996

For Rebecca and Rosamond

British Library Cataloguing in Publication Data.

Lawley, Ian
    Stoke-on-Trent in Old Photographs
    I. Title
    942.463

ISBN 0-7509-0249-3

Typeset in 9/10 Sabon.
Typesetting and origination by
Sutton Publishing Limited.
Printed in Great Britain by
WBC, Bridgend.

Contents

Foreword

Stoke-on-Trent is unique. It has a history and landscape like no other city. Before federation in 1910, it consisted of six separate pottery towns: Tunstall, Burslem, Hanley, Stoke, Fenton and Longton. Each of these towns still retains its own character and sense of identity. Unlike most of our large cities, Stoke-on-Trent remains the major centre of production for the industry on which it was founded. Although the skyline is no longer dominated by imposing rows of bottle ovens, the impact and importance of pottery manufacture is still abundantly evident in the local townscape.

The recent history of the Potteries has been one of rapid change. Coal-mining and steel-making, the other two principal local industries, have declined dramatically. As Stoke-on-Trent enters the post-industrial age, so its landscape is slowly evolving. The city has led the way in reclaiming derelict land. The waste heaps have gone or have been grassed over. Festival Park has risen from the ashes of the industrial past.

The photographic archive which is being developed at the City Museum and Art Gallery reflects these changes. It aims to create a permanent record of life in the Potteries during the recent past. A wide range of photographs has been collected, illustrating the local community at work and at play. Subjects include town and street scenes, houses and schools, factories and shops, leisure pursuits and civic activities. Many members of the local community have contributed to the archive, which is becoming an important educational resource. In its portrayal of aspects of the cultural and economic life of the city, it is also an exciting source of historical reference for local people.

Many people reading this book will, like myself, feel nostalgic for some vanished aspects of life in the city. Many will share the great sense of pride that Potteries people feel for their heritage. But we should not idealize the past. Looking at the photographs in this collection, we may also be glad that we are living now.

I am pleased that the interest of the museum service in recording the lives and experience of local people has found expression in this fascinating book. These remarkable photographs, most of them published here for the first time, give me enormous pleasure. I am sure that you will enjoy them too.

Councillor K. Alan Edwards
Chair, Museums, Arts and Heritage Committee
Stoke-on-Trent City Council

Introduction

As historical documents, photographs have an immediacy which cannot be matched by the written record. This compilation of photographs illustrates aspects of life in Stoke-on-Trent recorded by the camera since the 1870s. The images selected depict a wide range of subjects, reflecting some of the realities of living in a period of change. They do not present a complete or objective record. Rather they illuminate random fragments of the past, frozen on film for a fraction of a second; they may conceal as much as they reveal. Much of the day-to-day life of the Potteries has passed unrecorded. For example, there are no photographs in this collection showing women at work in their homes, cooking, cleaning and providing for their families. Only a few photographs depict industrial action. Oddly perhaps, in an area with a strong Labour Party tradition, there is little evidence of political activity.

The urban landscape of Stoke-on-Trent has been shaped unmistakably by industrial activity, particularly pottery manufacture. Detailed photographic records exist for some of the major pottery works, but many other local enterprises have gone virtually unrecorded. The remarkable diversity of trades and occupations is merely hinted at in the photographs which survive. Many photographs of people at work are taken from the employer's perspective, seeking to project a formal image of the workplace as a well ordered establishment. Yet the effects of long hours and hazardous conditions often show through on the faces of the working people pictured. In contrast, informal snapshots taken at work suggest the camaraderie that develops through shared experience. They have the immediacy that only personal involvement can bring.

Alongside the potbanks, factories, foundries, workshops and waste heaps were packed rows of working-class houses. It was an environment that bred disease. Cholera, diphtheria and scarlet fever were common complaints. During the 1897 diphtheria epidemic there were fourteen times as many cases of the disease in the Potteries than the national average. For a while, Longton had the highest rate of child mortality in England and Wales. The photographs in this collection of the John Street area suggest something of the conditions which prevailed.

A common recollection among older residents of the Potteries is the sense of community they felt as they were growing up. However poor their families may have been, people managed to amuse themselves. Home-grown entertainment was highly valued, all the pottery towns boasting well supported clubs, societies, choirs and sports teams. Again, the richness of experience is barely suggested in the photographic record.

Some of these images were taken by professional photographers, some by serious amateurs, while others are simply snapshots. Some are self-consciously posed or 'official' in nature, others are spontaneous celebrations of special occasions and holidays. Together, they offer a unique insight into the life of a community at work and play within the distinctive environment of the Potteries.

A community in celebratory mood. Families from the Trent Vale estate pose for a group photograph. The estate was built by the Sutton Housing Trust and completed in 1929.

SECTION ONE

Childhood

Girls at Dresden School, 1896. A National School was built at Dresden in 1866 to accommodate 293 boys, 215 girls and 210 infants. At this time boys and girls were separated into different classes. Separate entrances were provided.

Boys' class, Granville School, Cobridge, *c.* 1900. This school was opened in 1854 to provide elementary schooling for the children of iron and steel workers at the nearby Shelton Bar furnaces. Lessons were repetitive, with great emphasis placed on the three 'R's.

Class 3, Cooke Street School, *c.* 1904. Built by the Longton School Board in 1893, this large elementary school taught more than nine hundred pupils. Standing on the right is the headmaster, Mr Gibson.

Class 6, Middleport Senior School, 1932. Class photographs often offer an indication of the state of pupils' health and nourishment, and provide clues about the general standard of living in the school area.

PE lesson at Broom Street School, *c.* 1950. The areas provided for exercise and play were small. Girls and infants were allocated even less space than the boys.

Pupils at Broom Street School, Hanley, in their classroom, *c.* 1950. The first Board School to be built in Hanley, Broom Street School, was designed to accommodate around 720 children. Visiting the school in 1911, the inspectors commented that 'the happy and natural demeanour of the children is a pleasing feature'. Broom Street School closed in the early 1960s.

Speech Day at Brownhills High School for Girls, Tunstall, *c.* 1930. Brownhills opened in 1929 and like many new grammar schools adopted public school traditions. The first headmistress was Miss Willmot.

Pupils of Belmont Road Infant School, Etruria, *c.* 1934. The school had only recently opened. This group of children performing in the school yard was among its earliest intake. Jim Beeston (standing far left) recalls that it was a very happy school. He later became a governor.

School band, Carmountside, 1940. This photograph was taken for an album depicting life in the Potteries during wartime. Carmountside was chosen as being one of the most modern and well equipped schools in the city.

Ball Green Sunday School anniversary procession, 1950s. Each year Sunday school children would parade through the local streets, stopping at intervals to sing hymns.

Etruria Boys' Football Club, 1922. Members of the team pose proudly with the tournament shield and their players' medals at the end of a successful season. Rivalry between local boys' teams was often fierce.

Middleport School football team, 1934. The team poses for the camera with the Bartlett Cup, won in competition with other school teams.

Northwood Church of England School reserve football team, 1946. None of the boys could afford proper football boots. Roy Furnival (standing, second from left) recalls that some boys played in clogs, using rolled-up newspapers for shin pads.

Junior League champions, 1950/1, Broom Street School, Hanley.

Band of Hope tea, Hill Top, Burslem, 1937. The Band of Hope was an interdenominational organization set up to promote temperance and 'rational recreation' among working-class communities.

'The Beginners' Department,' Burslem Sunday School, 1937. The Methodist influence was strong in the Potteries and Sunday school played an important part in the lives of many children. In 1937 the Burslem Sunday School at Hill Top celebrated its 150th anniversary.

Church parade, 1940. Local Scouts form a guard of honour at St Bartholomew's church, Blurton.

Burslem Sunday School's 150th anniversary, 1937. The children pose in their anniversary outfits below Hill Top's imposing organ, which was given to the church in 1905 by Thomas Hulme JP.

Scouts at Kibblestone Camp, near Stone, 1940. The man standing on the far right is Ronald Copeland, who organized regular camps at Kibblestone.

Hill Top Cubs and Scouts, 1937, one of many troops attached to a local chapel.

Wellington Road School choir, Hanley Park, 1927. Singing competitions for schools were held in the park during the 1920s and '30s.

Local wakes outing, c. 1929. For those who could afford it, a day-trip by train or charabanc provided a welcome break from the industrial environment. However, many families had to make the best of local parks or the immediately surrounding countryside.

Children playing on a swing, possibly during wakes week, 1940. This photograph shows little evidence of the strains of wartime life.

'Keeping cool.' A group of Potteries children wade through a stream in the summer of 1940, oblivious of the momentous events taking place in the world outside.

Children playing on a see-saw, Etruria, *c.* 1950. The Shelton Bar steel works rises above the playing fields.

SECTION TWO
People at Work

An unusually large group of blacksmiths poses for a photograph outside an unidentified local forge, *c.* 1920. In 1900 there were around eighty smiths in the Potteries. As the use of working horses and ponies declined, the number of smithys dropped dramatically. By 1960 only ten smiths remained in Stoke-on-Trent.

Blacksmiths at work in the Moorland Road forge, Burslem, *c.* 1930. The bellows and hearth are visible on the left.

Colliery pit-head, probably Adderley Green, c. 1895. The mine at Adderley Green opened in 1799 and ceased production in 1934. It remained open for a while after this as a 'pumping pit' for the nearby Mossfield Colliery.

An unidentified surface worker at the Hulme Colliery, near Bucknall. This was one of around 144 mines being worked in north Staffordshire during the 1880s. Output stood at around four million tons. By 1900 it had risen to more than five and a half million tons.

In 1912 the Miners' Federation called a national strike to secure a minimum wage of 5s per shift for men and 2s for boys. This photograph, taken at the Florence Colliery, Longton, is one of a number depicting striking miners and their families picking coal from the tip.

Four miners walk along the Leek New Road in Cobridge on their way home from the Sneyd Colliery, 1929. There were no pit-head baths at this time. Sneyd Colliery was the last colliery to close in the Burslem area.

The Secretary of the Miners' Federation, Arthur J. Cook, arrives at Stoke-on-Trent during the General Strike of 1926.

A.J. Cook addresses a large crowd of north Staffordshire pit-men and their supporters. Cook, who rose to prominence in the South Wales district, coined the slogan: 'Not a penny off the pay, not a second on the day'. The strike ended in frustration and defeat.

Whitfield Colliery pit-head baths, 1937. Two very clean figures emerge from the baths which were provided by the colliery welfare committee as part of a drive to improve facilities. The staff canteen was opened at the same time. The men paid sixpence a week to use the baths.

'Snappings.' Mining trainees pose outside the Kemball Training Centre at Mount Pleasant, Fenton, 1950. Many of these lads are wearing compressed cardboard safety helmets. The two boys in the foreground are holding their snap tins. At this time more than fifteen thousand men were still employed underground in north Staffordshire. A central training scheme was set up at Kemball in 1946.

A wooden tower on wheels, erected in Hall Brothers' yard in Moorland Road, Burslem, in 1893. Designed for overhead work on electric trams, this tower was built for the British Electric Traction Company. Originally wheelwrights, Hall Brothers worked as coach builders during the early years of this century.

Interior of Shelton steel works, c. 1963. Iron and steel was produced and milled at Shelton Bar from the 1840s onwards. By the end of the nineteenth century three thousand people were employed on the site. The steel plant closed down in 1978.

A railway crane lifts a vertical support beam into place during reconstruction work on the Scotia Bridge, Tunstall, in the mid-1920s. The bridge carried the Potteries Loop Line on its way from Burslem to Tunstall station. At this time there were still as many as fifty trains a day using the line.

Scotia Bridge reconstruction, 1927. A small crowd gathers to watch one of the main supports being lowered into place. A LMS 0-6-2 tank engine and its brake van can be seen on the right of the picture.

LMS civil engineers supervise work on the reconstruction of the Scotia Bridge in 1927. Cross members are stacked in the two flat wagons in the foreground.

Harold Sergeant puts the finishing touches to a wooden crate in the yard at China Street, Fenton. For many years crate-making was an important subsidiary craft in the Potteries. Around fifty crate-makers were active in the area at the turn of the century, but by 1958 only fifteen yards remained open.

A crate-maker prepares materials at a yard off Brocksford Street, Fenton, 1949.

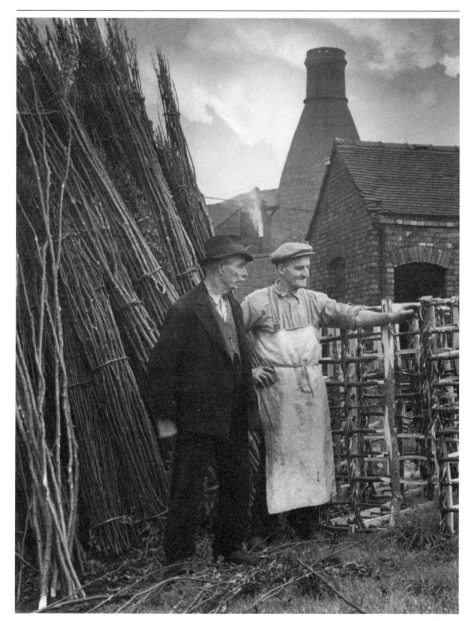

'Carriage is an extra.' This photograph, showing two crate-makers at work in Brocksford Street, off King Street, Fenton, was taken by Charles Trelfa in 1949. It was shown in the 'Changing Face of the Potteries' exhibition held at the Hanley Museum in Pall Mall in November 1950. Charles Trelfa was secretary of the Stoke-on-Trent Camera Club for twenty-one years. This image was processed and printed by his wife.

Workers at Henry Jackson and Son's yard in Sandbach Road, Cobridge, *c.* 1923. A well known local firm of coopers and case-makers, the business was maintained by three generations of the Jackson family.

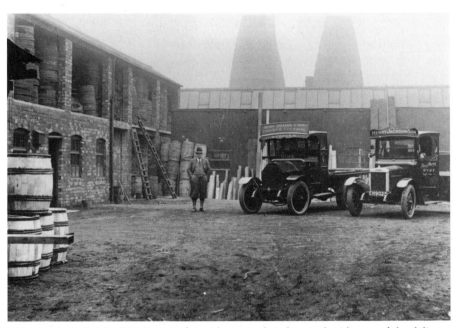

Henry Jackson (1866–1948) poses for a photograph in his yard with two of the delivery wagons.

These two men are pictured at work in the case-making shop at Henry Jackson's Sandbach Road premises.

Three coopers at work in the barrel shop at Henry Jackson's yard, 1923. The business had begun as a cooper's, expanding into case-making during the early years of the century.

A workman uses a hackle to help shape the bristles of a brush at Robert Sherwin's works, Lower Mollart Street, Hanley, *c*. 1970. This particular tool is now in the collection of the City Museum and Art Gallery, Stoke-on-Trent.

One of Sherwin's employees prepares brush heads, *c*. 1970. Sherwin's brush-making factory was housed in a former pottery, the Smithfield works, most of which survives.

Oswin Willcox poses for a photograph with his horse and delivery wagon, *c.* 1900. His bakery was situated at 17 Bethesda Street, Hanley.

An ice-cream seller poses with his hand-cart in a Potteries street. A number of Italian families settled in the area during the 1930s, setting up as ice-cream makers.

Packing margarine at Siddall Brothers' warehouse. A huge variety of produce was available from this wholesale grocery warehouse, which was established in Wesley Street, Fenton, by the early 1920s. Described as 'manufacturing confectioners, wholesale grocers and provision merchants', Siddall's packaged their own groceries as well as handling familiar branded products such as Quaker Oats and Sunlight soap.

Two young men pack self-raising flour at Siddall Brothers' warehouse.

Preparing groceries for despatch at Siddall Brothers' warehouse.

Clerical staff at work in the general office, Siddall Brothers' warehouse.

Trading Standards Officer, *c*. 1960. This photograph was taken by the City of Stoke-on-Trent Weights and Measures Department as a promotional image. In 1974, with local government reorganization, responsibility for trading standards passed to Staffordshire County Council.

Postal workers, Burslem Post Office, at the turn of the century. The main post office in Burslem was sited at the corner of the Market Place. At this time there were four deliveries and six collections a day.

This unusual photograph shows staff at work in the wages office at Hanley Town Hall in around 1905. Within a few years, the Borough of Hanley had ceased to exist. In 1910, the six Potteries towns of Tunstall, Burslem, Hanley, Stoke, Fenton and Longton were linked together to become Stoke-on-Trent. City status followed in 1925.

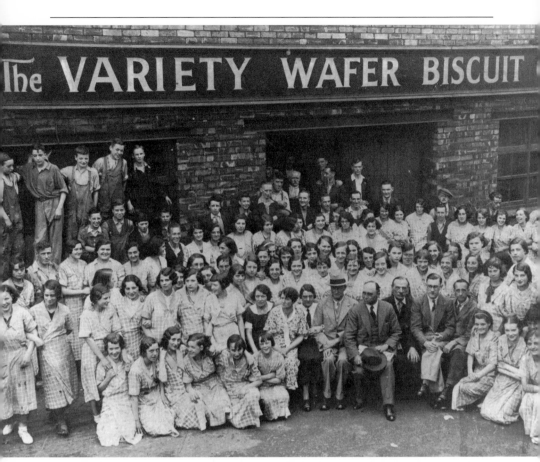

The Variety Water Biscuit Company was established in 1910 by J.W. Brooks and was originally situated in Hope Street, Hanley. When this photograph was taken in 1936 the factory had moved to Bryan Street, having just been sold by Mr Bell, seated in the hat, to Mr Foskie on his left. This image depicts the whole workforce: the young boys at the back who worked in the tinning shop, the men from the maintenance team to the right at the back, the women who worked as bakers in the centre, and the young girls at the front who packed the wafers for transportation. The cornets and wafers made by Variety were exported to America.

SECTION THREE
Potbanks

In 1913 King George V visited Alfred Meakin's Royal Albert Works in Tunstall. The following sequence of photographs was taken at this time. These are the enamel kilns.

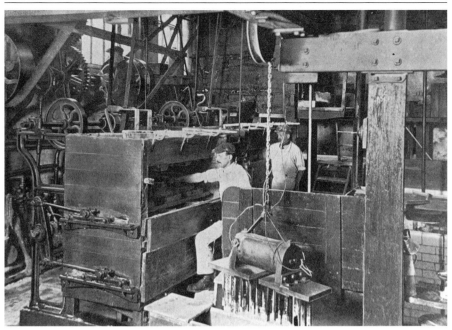

Two of Meakin's workmen mix the raw clay. A complicated system of belts and pulleys was used to drive the machinery.

Making vegetable dishes. The boy on the right is preparing sheets of clay which the adult workers would then press into moulds.

Saggars are filled with glazed ware prior to firing in the glost oven.

Workmen fill saggars with clayware, before placing in the bisque oven. The ware was placed in silica sand inside the saggar.

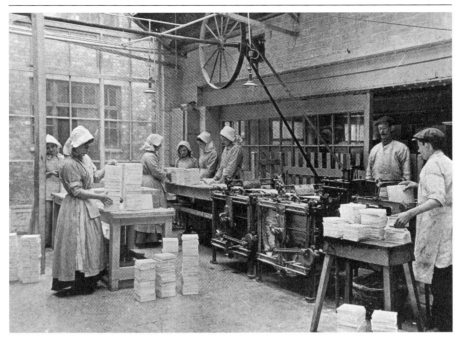

Glazing white tiles by machinery.

Packers place the finished pots in straw inside large wooden crates, ready for shipment to every part of the world.

Interior of the engine house at an unknown pottery factory, *c.* 1905. The engine-man is standing alongside a horizontal steam engine, which is driving a small generator. Steam power was used throughout the pottery industry to drive a variety of processes, using belts, pulleys and ropes. The engine house seems unusually clean.

Selectors in a pottery warehouse, *c.* 1905. The exact location of this works is unknown.

A group of pottery workers, possibly placers, pose for a photograph in the yard of an unidentified potbank.

An unusual studio photograph showing three male pottery workers in their working clothes. Like many working people in the Potteries at this time, they are wearing clogs.

This informal photograph shows a group of women pottery workers at the 'clay end' of a factory. Such women enjoyed lower status than those employed in the decorating shops.

Women workers, possibly fettlers, removing ware from moulds and placing it on drying racks, at Furnival's works, 1920. It is possible that, in the aftermath of the First World War, these women were undertaking work traditionally done by men.

Ware placed in a muffle kiln for firing. Although electric kilns were introduced in the late 1920s, coal continued to be used to generate heat for pottery manufacture until the '60s.

A kiln fire-man stacks ware in an enamel kiln at the Enoch Wedgwood works in Tunstall, 1923. Such kilns provided a lower temperature, which allowed delicate decoration to be applied to the work.

Johnsons tile works, Tunstall, *c.* 1906. New tile presses had just been installed when this photograph was taken. Clay dust was pressed to form the tiles which were then set to dry before firing.

Tile-making workshop. Tiles are sorted by women operatives before firing in the bisque oven.

A fettler prepares hollow vessels at the W.T. Copeland works in Stoke, *c.* 1949. This photograph is one of a sequence taken by Charles Trelfa to record pottery-making techniques in the mid-twentieth century.

A thrower at his bench in the Copeland works, *c.* 1949. Traditional skills and levels of craftsmanship remained essential for the pottery industry.

Fettlers at work, making soup cups, at the Copeland works. In 1970 the name of the factory was changed to Spode.

A pottery worker making pots on a jolley at the Dudson Brothers' factory, Hanover Street, Hanley.

William Thomas Vickers at work in the Sanitary Pottery at Longport, now demolished. This unusual self-portrait was taken by Mr Vickers, a keen member of the Hanley Camera Club and the Society of Staffordshire Photographers, in the 1940s.

Serving the Community

Nursing staff at the City General Hospital, London Road, Stoke, 1925.

Patients and nurses pose for the camera in the geriatric ward at the City General Hospital, 1925. The ward occupied what had been the old workhouse on London Road, Stoke.

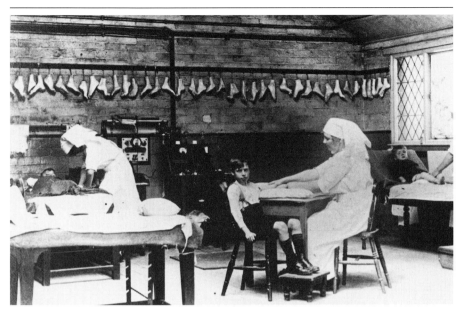

Nurses treat children with bone deformities at the Orthopaedic Hospital, Hartshill, in 1925. Ranged around the wall are casts of children's deformed feet. The casts were made so that the hospital cobbler could fashion the right corrective footwear for each child.

Christmas at the Orthopaedic Hospital, 1925. All the children kept in at the hospital over Christmas were brought together for a party in the casting room. Sprigs of holly are nestled among the foot casts as decoration.

Moorville Hall, near Weston Coyney, *c.* 1916. During the First World War, the hall was used as a convalescent hospital for soldiers invalided home from the trenches. Three servicemen and a female passenger sit in a car, while staff pose fixedly for the camera.

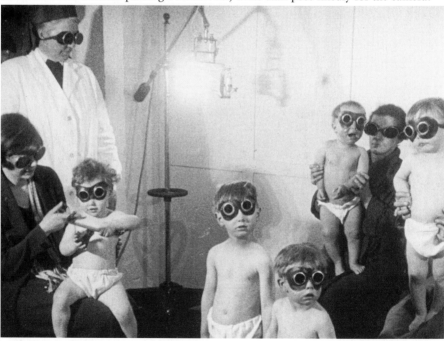

This photograph is a still from the 1926 film detailing the activities of Stoke-on-Trent Corporation. The children are probably being treated for rickets or other nutritional disorders. The ultraviolet rays which helped the children produce the vitamins necessary for healthy growth were so bright they had to wear special goggles. The treatment room was in the City General Hospital.

Street cleaners set out for work early one morning in 1926.

Road repairs at Snow Hill, Shelton, 1926. City Council workmen prepare the ground for repairs on this busy route between Stoke and Hanley.

The first motor fire-engine to be used in the Potteries was brought into service in 1917. Before 1925 there were six fire brigades in the district with little coordination between them. In that year the brigades were centralized to provide a more effective service.

The crew of a motor fire-engine, Longton fire station, 1935. From 1925 the city was divided into three areas with fire stations in Hanley, Burslem and Longton. The Longton brigade comprised one officer, five permanent firemen and five part-time firemen. The houses of the firemen were connected to the station by call bells.

The funeral of Corporal W. Merry of the Longton Volunteer Fire Brigade passes New Street. Merry died attending a fire on 24 March 1903.

The Lodge, Queen's Park, Longton, *c.* 1890. The first public park in the Potteries, laid out on land given by the Duke of Sutherland, Queen's Park opened in July 1888. The Lodge, designed in the half-timbered Queen Anne style, was the home of the park superintendent.

Walkways at Queen's Park, *c.* 1890. Three miles of walks were laid out, together with an impressive carriage drive. More than fifteen thousand trees and shrubs were planted in the park which the Duke of Sutherland claimed would provide a reservoir of clean air amid the smoke of the Potteries.

The bridge, Queen's Park, *c*. 1890. The man standing on the bridge is believed to be John McPhail, who was appointed park superintendent in July 1888. At first, he was paid 30s a week, with rent, rates, taxes, coal and gas provided free. His salary was increased to 35s in 1890, rising to £2 in 1891.

The lake, Queen's Park, *c*. 1890. A man, probably John McPhail, and a boy pose on board a raft.

A summer afternoon in Queen's Park, *c.* 1900. Although many children used the park, no special provision was made for them at this time. In 1899, for instance, it was resolved not to install swings or provide cricket and football pitches.

The Lake, Queen's Park. The lake was stocked with perch, roach, carp and trout, but was described as 'scarcely deep enough to drown the most diminutive individual who may perchance to fall therein'.

The boating lake, Hanley Park, *c.* 1900. During the 1890s an innovative young landscape architect, Thomas H. Mawson, was commissioned to transform 80 acres of derelict land into a public park. The ornamental lake, fed from the canal, cost £2,500 to construct.

Children at Hanley Park Horticultural Fête. School parties were brought to the annual fête in the hope that a visit to the flower tents would instil a disposition towards seeking improvement through leisure. Pupils were encouraged to enter their own home-grown plants for the children's competition.

Minton Memorial Building, Stoke-on-Trent, *c*. 1960. Designed to accommodate the Schools of Art and Science previously housed in the Town Hall, the Minton Memorial Building was constructed in 1858. Public baths were erected immediately behind the building and opened in 1861. Access to the baths was provided via the passageway between the library (far left) and the Memorial Building.

The Free Library (left) and the School of Art (centre), London Road, Stoke, 1890. Designed by Charles Lynam and built on a site given by Colin Minton Campbell at a cost of £2,850, the library opened in 1878. It also housed the museum collections of the Potteries Athenaeum. The round pillars and iron railings were removed in the 1950s. The range of buildings beyond the School of Art was Minton's Earthenware Factory.

Hanley Museum, Pall Mall, *c.* 1930. The North Staffordshire Technical, Art and Industrial Museum was opened in the former Mechanics Institution in Pall Mall in 1890. Its aim was to promote 'skill in workmanship, beauty in design and economy in production'. In 1927 the museum was extended to include an art gallery.

Natural History Gallery, Hanley Museum. In 1908 the collections of the North Staffordshire Field Club were given a permanent home in the Hanley Museum. The new gallery was opened by the locally born scientist Sir Oliver Lodge. Among the most striking exhibits were the heads of two cattle from Chartley.

End of an era. The upper storey of the original City Museum and Art Gallery is demolished, following the opening of the new museum in 1956. The structure had become unsafe, prompting the move to the new site.

The City Museum and Art Gallery, Hanley, 1956. In August 1953, following a twenty-five year campaign, it was finally agreed to build a new museum to house the city's priceless ceramics collections. Built on the site of the Bell Pottery, on the corner of Bethesda Street and Broad Street, the new museum opened in October 1956. It had cost £46,000.

SECTION FIVE

Shops and Pubs

By 1900 John Siddall had opened grocery stores in both Heron Street and King Street, Fenton. An impressive array of products is piled high in the window.

Hulson's delivery vans before their early morning rounds. Frost is still on the roofs and the ground. Hulson's was a well known Longton firm. Established in 1871, the business moved to Vale Street in the first decade of the twentieth century, where it became a wholesale outlet. When this photograph was taken it still had shop premises. The confectionery staff can be seen to the left of the delivery vans.

A small general store at Longport. This shop was run by Mrs Wellings and then by her daughter. The wall above the shop window is dominated by an advert for Swan Vestas matches. The photograph was taken by the shopkeeper's son-in-law, William T. Vickers.

Elijah Derricott's fish shop, *c.* 1910. The staff pose for a group portrait on the pavement in Hanley High Street (now Town Road). The 'fried fish' trade in the Potteries began during the 1880s when three shops opened in Burslem. The trade took off during the following decade. By 1896 there were fifty-one fish and chip shops in the area, providing a convenient source of nourishment for families in which both the mother and father worked long hours. Kelly's 1924 *Potteries Directory* lists 261 fish and chip shops, sixty-three of which were in Hanley alone.

Alfred Austin's tobacconist shop was situated at the top of the High Street in Stoke. One of more than a hundred tobacconists in the Potteries listed in 1904, it had closed by 1932.

W.B. Jones' tobacconist and sweet shop. Two local characters pass the time of day outside the small corner shop.

Brassington Bros established their first shoe shop in 1901. By 1924 they had opened three shops in Hanley – in Tontine Square, Parliament Row and Broad Street.

Brassington Bros' shoe shop in Campbell Place, Stoke, was established by the early 1920s and closed in 1968. The premises were subsequently occupied by Dewhursts.

Brassington Bros display their footwear at the County Show, Longton. An enormous pair of Dunlop wellington boots enjoys pride of place. Left to right: Mr E. Brassington, Mr Woodcock, Lewellyn Farrington.

J. Blagg was established as a draper and milliner at 63 Stafford Street in Hanley by 1880. This photograph, which also shows H.J. Mills' fruit and vegetable store, was taken in around 1890.

James Goodson and Son established a boot-making and shoe-retailing business in Tontine Square in 1891. Within a few years, the firm had moved to these larger premises on the opposite side of the square. With its double-fronted window display, the shop enjoyed a prominent position on the corner of the square. Goodsons stocked everything from heavy walking boots to satin slippers, and imported fashionable lines from Paris, Vienna and other continental centres. Four generations of the Goodson family worked in the shop, which is now occupied by the travel agents, Lunn Poly.

A policeman looks on as improvement work takes place on Bratt and Dyke's department store in Trinity Street, Hanley. Oliver Bratt and Henry Dyke acquired this site in 1896, demolishing the Roebuck Inn to build a large, three-storey store. The premises included accommodation for shop assistants, who were required to take a weekly bath and attend church or chapel regularly. The store closed in 1989.

More than a hundred people queue for the start of a sale at Naylor's Bon Marche in Tunstall during the 1950s. On the right of the picture, attached to a lamp-post, can be seen a sign for Tunstall station.

Crown Bank Hotel, Hanley, *c.* 1890. This three-storey building on the left of the picture now houses the Midland Bank. The inn on the right was the Marquis of Granby, now demolished.

John Dobson opened a camera shop in Hope Street, Hanley, during the 1920s. By the 1950s, when this photograph was probably taken, the shop had moved to Broad Street.

The Market Square in Hanley has been used for selling produce by market gardeners and other traders for around two hundred years. At the top of the square stood the Angel Hotel and the Grapes Hotel, both of which were demolished in the mid-1960s and replaced with a new row of shops.

The Market Hall in Hanley was built in 1849 and demolished in the 1980s to make way for the Potteries Shopping Centre. The archway in the centre of the building was the entrance to the market.

Swan Passage, Hanley, *c.* 1920. A fish market was held in a hall adjoining Swan Passage from the mid-nineteenth century until the mid-1920s.

A man and a boy stand outside The Trumpet Inn in Hanley. In 1900 the landlord was Charles Merriman.

The Cliffe Vale Inn, *c.* 1925. The landlord, Fred Myatt, and staff stand in front of this beer-house in Shelton Old Road, Stoke. Note the advertising signs for Oxo in the windows.

The Waterloo Inn, *c.* 1890. The public house, offering warmth, companionship, bright lights and beer, was an important social focus. Until 1899 it was common for working people to be paid at their 'local'.

The former Castle Inn, Uttoxeter Road, Longton, 1974. In around 1940 this long-established public house was converted into shop premises for an electrical firm, Vass and Co.

Working for the Co-op

Birches Head Co-op and Post Office. The Burslem Industrial Co-operative Society was set up in 1900 and opened its first shop the following year. The Birches Head branch opened in 1907 and there were soon shops throughout the Potteries. By 1922 the society had a membership of 28,975 people.

Co-op shop number one, *c.* 1924. The Burslem Industrial Co-operative Society's first shop was situated on Newcastle Street, Burslem. All Co-ops had the same staff structure: delivery boy (on the left), grocery assistants, a 'first hand' (who was like an assistant manager), and a shop manager. There was also a confectionery manager and a butcher. Sid Sweatmore, the butcher at the Burslem Co-op, stands third from the right, hands on hips.

The Smallthorne Co-op, in Ford Green, 1928. Mr Bateman, second from the left, was 'first hand' at the Smallthorne shop before becoming manager of the Vivian Road Co-op.

The Vivian Road store. This shop was part of the Burslem Co-operative and was opened in 1933. Mr Bateman, to the right in front of the doorway, was the manager. The women on the far right of the photograph are the staff of the confectionery department.

Co-op managers' charabanc outing, 1933. Every year the managers of the Burslem Co-operative Society went on an annual working weekend. They would visit the various CWS factories and warehouses, sampling the goods and produce they sold all year. The weekend also provided an opportunity for shop managers to socialize and talk about mutual concerns. This group of managers is photographed on board a solid-wheeled charabanc.

Co-op Dairies milkmen. This group photograph was taken in 1929 at the time of the opening of the new Co-op Dairy on Shelton New Road.

Horse-drawn dairy carts standing outside the new Co-op Dairy, *c.* 1930. Within a year of opening, the dairy began to supply local schools with milk on the recommendation of the medical profession.

Walter Gregory in the street with a hand-cart laden with milk bottles.

Bill Broxton, with horse and dairy cart. Several of the photographs in this sequence were taken by Mr Broxton.

Dairywoman, late 1940s. Women were employed on the milk delivery rounds during the Second World War and the years which followed until the servicemen returned. This photograph was taken in an area of poor housing. Outside toilet blocks can be seen on the left, unusually at the front of a row of houses rather than at the back.

G. Fradley and horse, late 1940s. The bulky document in Mr Fradley's pocket is his round book. This was used to keep a record of deliveries.

Riding pillion. Co-op dairymen pose with a Triumph Sunbeam motorcycle. The man on the far right is holding metal delivery crates.

Co-op Dairy vans and their drivers line up outside the Shelton New Road depot, *c.* 1930. Almost all the delivery vans used by the Co-op in the '30s were Ford Model As. The Co-op had its own body shop to customize the vehicles for each specific task, from transporting meat to carrying milk.

Two Co-op milkmen enjoy some horseplay in the dairy yard during the winter of 1950.

Young Co-op dairymen, late 1940s. They are posing against a horse-drawn milk float.

A Co-op milkman on his round with an electric milk float from the Sneyd Green depot, probably during the late 1960s. Customers paid for their milk in advance, buying checks which were placed on the doorstep and collected by the milkman on delivery.

Houses and Homes

Century Street, Hanley, *c.* 1890. The dominance of the pottery industry created an environment that was even less healthy than that of most other industrial towns.

Milner Street, off Bethesda Street, Hanley, during the late 1940s. Substantial areas of closely built and poorly lit housing still remained, many without baths or indoor lavatories. These houses were demolished in 1958.

Children stand self-consciously as a City Council photographer records their street. A housing committee had been set up in 1919, and during the late 1920s the local authority conducted extensive housing surveys in preparation for slum clearance.

Young lads, 'round the entry', 1920s. This is a typical back alley, lined with outside toilets.

Main John Street, 1928. The John Street area was a number of streets set back from the High Street, Longton. The following sequence of photographs was taken by the Corporation's Housing Department to make a case for including John Street on the list of clearance areas. John Street was demolished in 1935, but up to that time was a vibrant, if infamous, community.

Court number one, behind Upper John Street. Although the housing was some of the worst in the city, the people who lived in John Street regularly whitewashed their walls, even after the area was scheduled for demolition. Behind the streets were courts like this one where outside toilets and pigeon lofts competed for space. In 1933 eight people lived in the two-roomed house nearest the camera.

The back of Middle John Street. In this photograph you can see how saggars have been used to form a wall in the back yard. The area was dominated by the pottery factories which surrounded the small houses.

The back of Middle John Street. The houses had no gas or electricity. The only running water was a tap shared by up to ten people in the back yard. The outside toilets were also shared by two or three families.

Two women stare back at the photographer as he records their street. The women lived in Broddy's Row. Built in the 1830s, like much of the John Street area, the row comprised five cottages with two rooms on the ground floor and two upstairs. In 1935 when the area was demolished, Broddy's Row was left standing.

Meirhay Road looking north east over the Shraf Ruk. The Shraf Ruk was an area of waste ground where local pottery factories discarded broken and surplus ware. It was used as a playground by the children of John Street and a venue for illegal gambling by the men of the area.

A pottery worker walks home from Myott's works along Crane Street in Cobridge, 1930. Crates for packing pottery are stacked on the pavement outside the works. The terraced houses, built close to the factory buildings, are typical pottery workers' homes.

St Anne's Street, Hanley, *c.* 1950. Some of the houses in the street have been demolished, leaving an area of waste ground.

Hanley Road housing scheme, looking north from the Sneyd Arms, 1920s. In the years following the First World War the council began an extensive programme of house building. More than eight thousand council-houses were built between 1921 and 1939.

Cottages at Vinebank Street, Stoke-on-Trent, 1960. These cottages remained gas-lit until they were eventually demolished. The street had been known as Vine Street until 1959.

Young mother with pram, Etruria Vale, *c.* 1955. This photograph was taken on the corner of Sun Street.

Backs of houses, Goldenhill Road, Longton, *c.* 1980. At this time, almost fifteen thousand homes in the city still lacked at least one basic amenity. Most of these were privately owned.

Belgrave Road, Dresden, *c.* 1920. The residential suburb of Dresden was developed during the 1860s and '70s, largely by the Longton Building Society. For a brief period Dresden was an independent district with its own board of health, but it was absorbed into the Borough of Longton through an Act of Parliament in 1883.

Longton Hall, Blurton. John Myatt, aged 6, stands in front of Longton Hall, where his family lived. The Myatts were farmers who came from Stone. They bought Longton Hall and the Top Farm in Blurton where John grew up and later worked. Soon after this photograph was taken the hall was converted into flats. It was condemned in the 1920s.

Stoke-on-Trent at War

Stoke railway station, Winton Square, *c.* 1918. The station has been decorated in support of the military alliance. The insignia of the North Staffordshire Railway Company is given pride of place above the Union Jack.

First World War tank no. 119, Market Square, Hanley. A large crowd is encouraged to buy war bonds during 'Tank Week' in 1918. Towns and cities throughout the country vied with each other to translate patriotism into financial support through the purchase of bonds.

Stoke Labour Exchange Civil Defence Volunteers, *c.* 1940. Many thousands of local people gave up their spare time to make a contribution to the war effort.

St John Ambulance workers with Red Cross baskets prepared for prisoners of war. In the centre stands a representative of the LMS railway company which transported the baskets from Stoke station.

Bomb damage to houses, *c.* 1942. Although Stoke-on-Trent did not suffer heavy bombing, damage to property around the city was caused by stray clusters. The danger of air raids was taken very seriously. A number of people who failed to make proper black-out arrangements were brought before local courts, and one man was imprisoned by magistrates.

Rescue workers survey the damage to housing in May Bank following a bombing raid, 1941. A huge crater has opened up in the foreground.

ARP workers inspect bomb damage to houses in Porthill, 1941. The house on the left has collapsed.

This removal van belonging to J.H. Kelsall was destroyed by a stray bomb in 1942. Luckily no one was hurt in this freak incident.

Wreckage at the new nurses' home, North Staffordshire Royal Infirmary, 1940. Two days after the home was opened it was destroyed by a stray bomb. An operating theatre was wrecked during the same raid.

Soldiers enjoy free tea and sandwiches at Stoke station, 1942.

Cadets on manoeuvres, 1943. Boys from 237 squadron of the ATC carry their kit into Stoke station on their way to training camp.

The lord mayor of Stoke-on-Trent admires a portrait of Joseph Stalin. This image was included in a book of photographs commissioned by the City Council to show solidarity with the people of the Soviet Union in the Second World War. The book was never sent to the USSR and was forgotten. It remains a fascinating document of the city's life in wartime. The photographs that follow in this section have all been taken from the book.

The importance of coal for the war effort meant that miners remained in their jobs and were not conscripted. A nutritious diet was regarded as essential for their work.

Land Army girls. In total war everyone had a role. Around ninety thousand young women, many from towns and cities, volunteered to work on farms in the place of men who had been called up to join the forces. If they were attracted by the recruiting posters, which presented a romantic picture of the country life, the reality was different – hard work, long hours and prejudice against their taking on men's work.

Two turkeys prepare to make their sacrifice for the war effort.

Hanley 'invaded'. Light tanks parade along Parliament Row, Hanley, *c.* 1941.

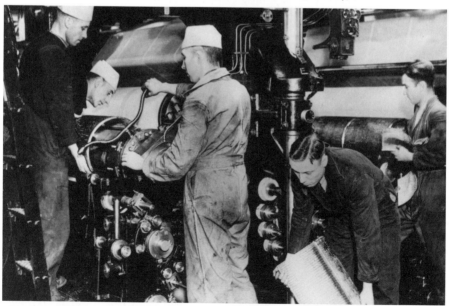

The printing presses at the *Evening Sentinel* newspaper offices, 1942. Throughout the war the presses at the *Sentinel* kept rolling at Northcliffe House, Foundry Street. The paper maintained its distribution throughout Staffordshire and Cheshire.

Washing up in the fresh air: Scouts clear up after eating a healthy meal while the lord mayor and lady mayoress look on. Kibblestone Camp, where this photograph was taken, was a regular site for the Scouts. The camps were often organized by scoutmaster Ronald Copeland (standing, third from right).

Girls dancing in Hanley Park during a spring festival, *c.* 1940.

Exercise class, Carmountside School, 1940. Boys are put through their paces in the school gym.

Boys' craft class, Carmountside School. Carmountside was photographed for the album because it was a modern, purpose-built school.

Decorating the ware. Paintresses were the aristocrats of the decorating shop, which was always seen as superior to the 'clay end' where the pots were made. These paintresses are working at Wedgwood's new Barlaston factory. This photograph was taken in March 1940, shortly after the factory opened.

Women pottery workers walking into work at the new Wedgwood factory, 1940. The new site was in a village far from the centre of town, and surrounded by fields.

Ernest Bevin meets Stoke City players. In 1941 Bevin, who was Minister for Labour in Churchill's coalition government, attended the match between Stoke City and Manchester City. He was introduced to the players by Harry Booth. The players are, left to right: Edwin Blunt, Stan Glover, Billy Mold, Syd Peppit, Tommy Sale, -?-, Frank Soo. Stoke City won the match 5–0.

SECTION NINE
Wakes and Weekends

Wakes fair in St John's Square, Burslem, in the late 1880s. Burslem wakes were traditionally held during the last week of June. An attempt to establish a single wakes celebration for the Potteries in 1879 was short-lived. Following a ballot of Burslem rate-payers it was resolved to re-adopt the traditional wakes week after only a year.

A family excursion, 1874. A well-to-do local family enjoys a day out in the countryside.

Boating on Rudyard Lake. This was a popular destination for Potteries pleasure seekers, particularly during wakes week.

Works outing, early twentieth century. Many local factories organized annual excursions for their workers and families. This photograph appears to have been taken in Church Street, Longton.

Family group with bicycles, *c.* 1895. Cycling was a popular activity for those who could afford it during the 1890s. Among the accessories available were special cyclists' corsets.

Charabanc outing, *c.* 1920. This photograph was taken outside the premises of Primrose Motor Coaches in Stoke Road, Shelton. The charabanc, a large open car full of seats, was a popular mode of transport for day-trips.

A novelty group portrait of six Potteries holiday-makers. This photograph was taken on the promenade at Blackpool, a popular destination for better-paid pottery workers.

A charabanc outing, *c.* 1925. This group of Potteries holiday-makers is about to set off on a day-trip to Llandudno.

Wakes week fun, 1950s. Young women enjoy the pleasures of the fairground in Regent Road, Hanley. This site remained the focus for annual festivities until the 1960s. 'It was our holiday, because we didn't go away,' recalls one resident of Ogden Road, whose home backed on to the fairground site. 'When it came near the wakes, we couldn't wait. We were all excited. We might have been going abroad.'

A curious picture, inscribed 'A.T. with bicycle'. The spring flowers around the handlebars seem to indicate that 'A.T' was dressed in this way for a spring festival. His clothes are covered with small decorated squares of fabric which he would have collected from cigarette packets. He has even used the packets themselves in places.

Skating rink, Hanley. This strangely eerie photograph shows the interior of the skating rink which stood in Albion Street in Hanley during the early years of the twentieth century.

Harry Wild with his bicycle at a race meeting, 1920s.

Afternoon refreshments, summer 1924. Members of the Potteries Cycle Club take a break for tea during a Saturday ride. Springing from working-class aspirations to leisure and social improvement, cycling clubs offered both camaraderie and an opportunity to breathe the clean air of the countryside.

The Potteries Cycle Club, 1923, one of many clubs that flourished between the wars. Members pose for a group portrait with their bicycles during an outing. Owning a bicycle provided mobility, and opportunities for leisure activity centred around clubs and weekend rides.

Two generations play cricket in the shadow of the Shelton iron and steel works. Iron and steel were manufactured at Etruria from the mid-nineteenth century onwards. By the 1950s, the works had expanded to dominate the skyline.

Winners of the Northwood and District Football League, *c.* 1905. Photographed by the Longton photographer Robert Lewis, this was probably a factory team. From the late nineteenth century onwards football was the game of ordinary people, played and watched by more local people than any other sport.

Stoke City Football Club, 1918. Stoke was one of the founder teams of the Football League in 1888, coming bottom at the end of the first season. Football culture has remained strong in the Potteries throughout the twentieth century.

Philemon Swift, the Burslem photographer, took this photograph of the Enoch Wedgwood & Co. Ltd football team in 1923. In that year the team was not only champion of the Amateur Works League, but was also joint holder of the National Council Cup. The team was made up of workers from all parts of the factory, from a kiln fire-man and mould-makers to office workers. The players are surrounded by officials from the Pinnox Street works in Tunstall.

Hanley High School for Boys football team and their coach pose for a group portrait, 1928. Mr Allman, who played as outside forward, is seated on the far left. He remembers that the team had to travel to their ground at Basford by bus, before trudging up the bank to the muddy pitch.

Port Vale players promote milk as a source of footballing energy in this publicity shot taken in around 1965. An area of land behind the Sneyd Green Dairy, owned by the Co-op, was used by Port Vale as a training ground. Apparently, the dairy supplied free milk for the players during training sessions.

Tunstall men's swimming team in the early twentieth century. Swimming was promoted as a means of building up the strength of the population. Tunstall Baths were opened in 1890.

Trentham Pool, 1935. Trentham Gardens, with its large outdoor pool, was a popular destination for local families.

Choirs from the Potteries gained national renown in the nineteenth century for their expert performances of complex choral works. The strong Methodist presence in Stoke-on-Trent, with its use of tonic sol-fa (a simplified musical notation), was the seedbed of a great musical tradition. This photograph shows the Hanley Glee and Madrigal Society in Hanley Park, 1906. Under the direction of John Cope (centre) the choir won many local and national competitions, including the National Eisteddfodd. They also performed at Windsor Castle before Edward VII.

The White Cliff Hall Band. At the beginning of the twentieth century there were many bands and orchestras in the Potteries. A triennial music festival was held in the Victoria Hall to provide a showcase for local talent.

Gertie Gitana, a well known music-hall artist. Born in Longport in 1888, she later moved with her family to Frederick Street, Hanley, where her mother kept a shop. A child prodigy, she made her music-hall debut at the age of 8. She first sang 'Nellie Dean', the song for which she was most remembered, when she was 16, and performed to acclaim at the Lyceum Theatre, London.

The Grand Theatre, Trinity Street, *c*. 1900. It was built in 1897 at a cost of £25, 000.

A.J. Crane, *c*. 1930. Mr Crane was the manager of the Grand Theatre when it was converted into a cinema in 1931.

Happy Days Concert Party, Hill Top, 1937. A group of young Methodists provided musical entertainment as part of a programme of special events organized to celebrate the centenary of Hill Top Methodist church.

Old Mother Riley (Arthur Lucan) and cast members pose outside the Odeon, Hanley, in May 1947. Riley was appearing at the Theatre Royal at the time.

Events

George V visits Alfred Meakin's Pottery, Tunstall, 1913. The King is clearly visible, but Queen Mary is hidden behind George V's companion. If you look closely, you can see her foot. The women lining the route worked as gilders and blue-banders in the decorating shop at Meakin's.

Swan Bank in Burslem, looking towards Waterloo Road, *c.* 1920. A ceremonial arch has been erected in preparation for the visit of Edward, the Prince of Wales.

A large crowd lines the roadway to await the arrival of the Prince of Wales in Swan Bank. The official photographer can be seen with his tripod towards the centre of the picture.

The car carrying the Prince of Wales draws up to the Burslem war memorial as the crowds are held back by police. The memorial was designed by William Mellor.

Tunstall Town Hall, 1897. The crowd has gathered to hear the address of the mayor of Tunstall in celebration of Queen Victoria's Diamond Jubilee.

A procession headed by a band winds its way along Tontine Street, Hanley. A policeman in the centre of the picture is directing the marchers toward the Town Hall.

St George's Day parade, Hanley, *c.* 1920. The Scout band leads a march along the High Street, past the Angel Hotel Wine Vaults.

Charles Street Wesleyan chapel, Hanley. A procession of carriages arrives at the chapel, as two coal wagons pick their way through the gathering congregation. This impressive chapel was built in 1819 and could accommodate 770 people. Despite strong competition from other denominations, it continued to attract an average congregation of 550 during the mid-nineteenth century.

St Saviour's church carnival float, Bradeley village, 1952. A hospital charity parade was held in the village each year. Bradeley was a thriving community, tucked away in a valley to the north-east of the city. Known as 'the last place on God's earth', the village was demolished in 1988.

Coronation celebrations in Clifton Street, 1953. Street parties were held throughout the Potteries to celebrate the coronation of Queen Elizabeth II.

In 1927 all the old people from Milton were invited on an outing organized by Mr Steel, the landlord of the Miners Arms. Mr Steel paid for a dinner held at the Sunday school on Bagnall Road. All the oldest residents of Milton are shown here, including the colonel (far right), who always led the Whit Monday procession.

Keele Carnival parade, Hanley, *c.* 1960. A reveller entertains the crowd with a send-up of civic authority. The University of Keele had opened in 1951.

The cenotaph, Kingsway, Stoke-on-Trent. A large crowd has gathered to honour the local servicemen killed in action during the First World War. The dignitaries have arrived in the three cars which can be seen in front of the Kings Hall. In the distance, smoke pours from a factory chimney in the Copeland works.

Funeral of Chief Fireman Charles Lockett, Commerce Street, Longton, 1912. His coffin was carried through Longton on a horse-drawn fire-engine. He had died attending a fire.

Celebrating peace at Blurton, 1919. Today Blurton is a large housing estate but in 1919 it was a small rural village. Despite its small size, Blurton lost many young men during the First World War. A party was organized to celebrate the signing of the peace treaty and almost everyone from the village was present. The food was served at table in the grounds of Blurton House which is just visible in the background.

Members of the North Staffordshire Trades and Labour Council, 1905. The Trades Union Congress was held at the Victoria Hall, Hanley, in September 1905, at the suggestion of Enoch Edwards, the President of the National Federation of Miners. The meeting was hosted by the North Staffordshire Trades and Labour Council, which had been formed in 1893 to provide an effective voice for local trade unionists.

The Hanley Horticultural Fête. The annual fête, which took place in July, attracted strong support from local manufacturers who saw it as an opportunity 'to stimulate the taste for decoration and beauty which the district of the Potteries has depended upon for its existence'. Gardening was seen as a more worthy leisure activity for working-class people than various other pursuits! The fête was held on Wednesdays and Thursdays.

A mishap in Hanley Park, 1920s. Taken during preparations for Hanley Flower Show, this photograph is inscribed on the reverse: 'Tent falling on William Poulson'.

'Opportunities for Sport and Travel.' This large marquee housed an Army recruitment display. The Territorial Army also demonstrated their equestrian skills in the horse ring, which was laid out by the lake.

Exhibitors in the children's section at the Hanley Flower Show display their certificates. Competition entry forms were distributed to all the local schools. Prizes were presented at the Victoria Hall.

Death and rebirth of the Theatre Royal. On the night of 2 June 1949, Hanley's Theatre Royal was almost completely destroyed by fire. A theatre had stood on the same site since 1841, when the entrepreneur and impresario Mr Elphinstone opened an entertainment hall. In 1951 the rebuilding of the present theatre was completed and it reopened with the musical *Annie Get Your Gun*.

Around the Six Towns

'One of the five towns,' *c.* 1950. This panoramic view, looking across North Street to Etruria Vale, was taken from Hartshill Bank. Before the Clean Air Act of 1950, the level of atmospheric pollution in the Potteries was acute. The title given to this photograph perpetuates Arnold Bennett's misleading term for the Potteries.

'Staffordshire Black Country,' *c.* 1950. A similar view, this picture was taken from higher up on Hartshill Bank.

'Burslem Skyline,' c. 1950. This photograph, showing the canal at Middleport, was taken by J.P. Delaney and shown in the 'Changing Face of the Potteries' exhibition in 1950.

Early morning in the Potteries. A young woman poses against the imposing backdrop of bottle kilns and chimneys. Before the Clean Air Act, there were more than two hundred bottle ovens in the city.

The Goss Falcon works, Sturgess Street, Stoke-on-Trent, 1937. The two bottle ovens on the right still stand within the present Portmerion works.

The horse-drawn tram *Justice*, c. 1880. A horse-drawn tram service between Hanley and Burslem was started in 1862. Steam-driven trams were introduced on this route in 1882, when the line from Longton to Stoke was extended. Arnold Bennett recalled that during his youth there had been 'only two trams, drawn by horses, travelling between Hanley and Burslem, twice an hour'.

A two-wheeled horse-drawn cart makes its way from Sneyd Colliery, with a cargo of coal for firing. Four-wheeled wagons were rarely used in the Potteries to carry coal.

Stafford Street, Longton, *c*. 1900. T.W. Davis' piano and organ store can be seen in the centre and J. Yates' veterinary infirmary is on the right.

The Wedgwood works, alongside the Trent and Mersey Canal, Etruria, 1929. At this time, canal horses were still a familiar sight on the tow-path.

The Market Square, Hanley, from Fountain Square, *c*. 1890. The large building with a classical frontage was the old Town Hall, built on the site of the former butter market in 1845. The building was occupied by Lloyds Bank from 1886, and was rebuilt in 1936.

Piccadilly, Hanley. This early photograph shows Piccadilly before it was developed as a busy commercial street. The Unicorn Inn can be seen on the left.

Crown Bank Hotel (centre), viewed from Stafford Street at the turn of the century. This is an unusually quiet view of what was normally a bustling area at the centre of the town.

The Bell & Nicholson works in Broad Street, Hanley, occupied part of the site on which the City Museum and Art Gallery now stands. Pottery works stood on this site from the mid-eighteenth century onwards. In 1922 the works was occupied by the Bell Pottery Company and G.M. Creyke and Son. It had fallen into disuse by the 1950s and was eventually demolished.

Shelton Farm, *c.* 1950. The tower of St Mark's church can just be seen behind the Swynnerton Pottery, on the right.

Cottages on the corner of Vine Street and London Road, Stoke-on-Trent, *c.* 1920. An open-top car can be seen on the right. Trams ran along this route until 1927.

The Grapes, Stoke-on-Trent, *c*. 1900. This alehouse stood on the corner of the London Road and the High Street, in what is now Campbell Place. The site is currently occupied by a video shop. The factory building on the right is the Copeland pottery works.

Campbell Place, Stoke, from London Road, *c*. 1955. The Newcastle branch of the Trent and Mersey Canal passed alongside the road and under the large building on the right. The original Wheatsheaf Inn can be seen at the top of the street.

Victoria Road, Fenton, *c.* 1915. The potbank on the right is the Minerva works, formerly owned by Charles James Mason, and demolished in the early 1930s. The small building on the left was a tram shelter provided by the Potteries Electric Traction Company. The drinking fountain was later removed to Fenton Park.

'Child scramblers for coal cart spillings.' This memorable image, taken many years earlier by the Longton photographer W. J. Blake, was displayed in the 'Changing Face of the Potteries' exhibition in 1950. It shows the Wharf Street area of Longton.

Samuel Radford's China works, City Road, Fenton. This photograph was taken early one morning in October 1950.

Trentham Road, Dresden, 1960s. A coach turns into Trentham Road from Belgrave Road, past the Lord John Russell public house.

St James' church, Longton, seen from Webberley Lane, *c.* 1900. Built by the Church Commissioners, St James' was consecrated in June 1834.

The Wesleyan Methodist chapel, Stafford Street, Longton, *c.* 1890. This brick-built chapel opened in the early 1840s and was replaced in the 1930s by the Central Methodist Hall.

The Primitive Methodist chapel, Mow Cop, *c.* 1900. Mow Cop had been the scene of the Primitive Methodists' first open-air prayer meeting in May 1807. This small chapel was one of a number built in the area. Mow Cop Castle, described as 'a place of great resort for pleasure parties in the summer time', can be seen on the hillside (far right).

The swimming pool at Trentham Gardens, *c.* 1938. Once the estate of the Duke of Sutherland, the richest man in the county, Trentham Gardens became a playground for people from the Potteries. Horse-riding, train rides and boating on the lake were, together with swimming in the large outdoor pool, some of the activities on offer. Regular dances were held at the ballroom and the New Year's Eve ball was the most lively in the region.

Winter scene, Trentham. In 1906 Stoke-on-Trent suffered one of its severest winters this century. These houses, then surrounded by deep snow, still stand today, close to the Trentham roundabout. The photograph was taken with a field camera, the plate being exposed for up to three or four seconds. The figure on the left has moved slightly and become blurred.

Canal people, Etruria, 1950. The importance of canals as a means of transporting pottery declined after the 1930s, although the network still provided a living for some carriers.

Two narrow-boats moor together on the Trent and Mersey Canal, off Whieldon Road, in 1950. The building behind is Winkle and Wood's Colonial Pottery.

Etruria Vale Road, looking towards the Shelton steel works, *c.* 1960. The two photographs on this page were taken by Edward Gater who made an extensive and personal record of the city through photographs.

Wasteland, *c.* 1960. Three boys walk across derelict land off Bedford Street overlooking the Caldon Canal with Shelton Bar in the distance.

Haymaking in Trentham, 1898. The man in the boater on the far right was Edward Hughes, who owned a smallholding on what is now the site of Beechfield Road in Trentham. As well as being hard work, haymaking was also a sociable occasion. Edward Hughes invited friends to help including Mr Clowes, a potbank owner, who is posed in the centre with the rake.

The source of the Trent, Biddulph. This was an intriguing destination for workers from the city on Sunday outings.

A promotional photograph of Siddall's delivery van at Little Moreton Hall.

Milk from Top Farm. The Myatt family owned Top Farm, which stood to the north of Longton Hall Road in Blurton. This photograph, taken around 1928, shows John Myatt, the farmer's son, with Mr Plimmer (left), a farm labourer, preparing to set off on a delivery round.

Acknowledgements

The majority of photographs in this book belong to the photographic archive of the City Museum and Art Gallery, Stoke-on-Trent. Our thanks are due to the many individuals who have given photographs to the collection.

Special thanks for permission to reproduce photographs go to Mr D. Jackson, Hugh Leese, Ray Johnson, Mrs C. Trelfa, Mrs C. Wood, the North Staffordshire Nursing History Group, and the Sutton Housing Trust.

We would also like to thank Mr Allman, Ted Bateman, Roy Furnival, Kathy Niblett, Allan Townsend, and Jim Worgan for information; Richard Weston for photographic work; Judith Billing and Julie Morrall for their word-processing skills; and all our colleagues at the City Museum and Art Gallery. Any errors are our own.